The Lines of Seth

A Brief History of Heresy

Minister Dante Fortson

The Lines of Seth
A Brief History of Heresy

Website: www.ministerfortson.com

ISBN 10: 1470008505
ISBN 13: 978-1470008505

All scripture quotations in this book are taken from the King James Version of the Bible except where noted. Words appearing in bold are the author's own emphasis.

First Edition. Printed in the United States of America

Published by: Impact Agenda Media

Table of Contents

Acknowledgements

First and foremost I want to thank my Lord and Savior Jesus (Yeshua) for allowing me to complete this, my fourth book. Next I want to thank my wife Jenelle and my mom Pastor Perryetta Lacy for listening to endless hours of new research, discoveries, and strange theories. I appreciate it. Finally I would like to thank the following people for all the love and support that I have received over the years: Brian Lacy, Derrius, Taneka Dickson, Stanford Greenlee, Kareem Muller, Sis. Mary, Sis. Norma, J Rich, Xavier Jackson, Kwon, Dori Lynn, King Wells, Keith Well, Doug Riggs, Connie Huft, Jim Wilhelmsen, Rob Roselli, Proof Negative, Steve Quayle, Chuck Missler, Grant Jeffrey, Marvin Bittinger, L.A. Marzulli, all of my Omega Hour guests, all of my readers, and the entire Ignited Praise Fellowship family. If I missed anyone by name, please believe it was not intentional. May God continue to bless and keep you all.

Introduction

The Lines of Seth Theory is one of the most important theories that appears in the Bible. It is so important because much of our understanding of the Bible, starting at Genesis 6, is dependent upon whether or not this theory is true.

My Inspiration

This book originally appeared as Chapter 3 in my book, As The Days of Noah Were, but it soon became apparent that there was much more to the theory that I failed to address. Over the past couple of years I have received quite a few emails asking me to approach the issue from a more in depth perspective that would be easier to discuss with pastors, other researchers, and church goers. This book is a response to those requests.

The Purpose

The purpose of this book is to thoroughly explore The Lines of Seth Theory, its origin, and how it ties into the Biblical narrative. My goal is to take the reader on a step by step Biblical process which will help them better understand the events that occurred in Genesis 6:1-4. By the time we reach the end of the book, the interpretation of the Genesis 6 events will be very clear to all of those that read until they reach the end.

Setting Aside Christian Bias

Often times it is hard to set aside our long held beliefs and look at things from an objective perspective. Honest research is about finding truth and not pushing a preconceived agenda. Simply put, this book is about discovering the truth according to what the Bible says. Those that are familiar with my work know that I believe in changing my beliefs to fit the Bible and not changing the Bible to fit my beliefs. Studying with that in mind allows us to stick to the truth of God's word regardless of how it may make us look to other Christians that prefer to adhere to tradition over scripture. It is in that spirit that I ask the readers of this book to set aside any preconceived notions and let the word of God guide you to the truth about this fascinating topic.

The Literal Interpretation

I am a literalist when it comes to scripture. I do not allegorize, spiritualize, or strip the text of meaning in order to fabricate a meaning that fits my preconceived notions. If scripture does not indicate that the subject is a dream, vision, parable, etc. I take a literal approach to interpretation. In this book, that is exactly what you will find.

The Strong's Concordance

I refer to the Strong's Concordance a lot because more times than not, it clarifies the majority of speculation on what the original authors may have meant. It is my opinion that anyone that is serious about studying scripture needs a Strong's Concordance to use in their studies.

In Closing

I would like to encourage all of my readers to adhere to Acts 17:11 and check everything that I write and compare it with scripture. If you are not checking behind me, you are not doing what you are supposed to be doing when it comes to studying the word of God. Always check behind anyone claiming to teach the word of God. It is the only way to ensure that you are not being conditioned to accept false doctrine. With that said, I pray that you enjoy this book and it helps you in your quest for truth.

God bless,

Minister Dante Fortson

Minister Dante Fortson

Chapter 1: The Lines of Seth Theory

There are several theories that are based around foundational points in scripture, that without which, much of the Bible does not make sense. The Lines of Seth Theory is one of these theories. Unfortunately, many churches will not approach the subject even in an in depth Bible study, but if asked, many will admit to holding a belief in The Lines of Seth Theory. The reason for this is because the alternative view is a highly controversial and highly disputed theory which has caused a rift between many mainstream churches and what are considered "fringe Christians". So what is The Lines of Seth Theory all about?

An Explanation of The Theory

Within the Bible there are stories, and it is within the contents of these stories that we sometimes find oddities. When these oddities are found, there is usually an attempt made to make it make sense. Sometimes these explanations are Biblical and sometimes they are based on nothing more than personal opinion and belief. The Lines of Seth theory is an attempt to explain an oddity within the story of Noah's flood (Genesis 6).

> "And it came to pass, when men began to multiply on the face of the earth, and daughters were born unto them, That the sons of God saw the daughters of men that they were fair; and they took them wives of all which they chose. And the LORD said, My spirit shall not always strive with man, for that he also is flesh: yet his days shall be an hundred and twenty years. There were giants in the earth in those days; and also after that, when the sons of God came in unto the daughters of men, and they bare children to them, the same became mighty men which were of old, men of renown." - Genesis 6:1-4

The entire theory is encompassed within these four verses. The purpose of the theory is to explain three key groups of people that appear within the story of Noah's flood:

- The sons of God.
- The daughters of men.
- The giants on the earth.

1

The Lines of Seth Theory is not just another theory of mild importance that we can overlook. The events in Genesis 6:1-4 are referenced over and over again throughout the Bible, which is why the contents of the story are so controversial, divisional, yet important.

A Summary of Events

To those that hold a belief in this theory, there is no question that there is a spiritual separation between the descendants of Cain and Seth. After the slaying of Abel, Cain was cursed, and left his home to dwell in the land of Nod. During this time Cain took a wife and began to produce offspring that many believe were also ungodly like their father.

According to Genesis 4:25, Seth was a replacement for the slain Abel. Because Seth's son Enos began to call upon the name of the Lord and Noah's family was spared from the flood, it is believed that Seth's line followed a righteous path like their father.

When we read Genesis 6:1-4, we find that the sons of God and the daughters of men have begun mixing, which according to the theory was forbidden by God. It is because of this indiscriminant mixing that the entire earth becomes corrupted and is ultimately wiped out by the flood in Noah's time.

Elements of The Theory

The first item that this theory seeks to address is who the "sons of God" really are. According to the Lines of Seth Theory, the phrase "sons of God" refers directly to the male descendants of Seth. According to the story in Genesis, it was the sons of God that began taking the daughters of men and producing offspring with them.

The next element of the story that the theory seeks to address is the phrase "daughters of men". The Lines of Seth interpretation is that the phrase "daughters of men" refers to the female descendants of Cain. According to the theory, it was these women that gave birth to the giants.

The final element that this theory seeks to explain is the existence of giants. Proponents of this theory usually believe that that God forbid Seth's line from marrying those in Cain's line, and that the unpermitted mixing caused genetic giants to be born. Throughout this book we are going to discover how this interpretation came about, why it is so important, and why the alternate theory is considered heresy.

The Alternative Theory

The Angel Theory is considered by the mainstream church to be heresy. This theory teaches that the sons of God were actually angels and the phrase "daughters of men" refers to mankind in general. Tradition teaches that angels are not capable of reproduction, and as a result the text in Genesis 6 cannot be a reference to angels. There are several very important men that were opposed to this theory:

- Cyril of Alexandria
- St. Augustine
- Sextus Julius Africanus
- Simeon Bar Yochai
- Thomas Aquinas

In the next chapter we will look at some of these men and find out why they took the position that they did concerning the events in Genesis 6.

The Breakdown

Now that the foundation for the Lines of Seth Theory has been laid and we know what the theory seeks to explain, we need to look into the history of the theory to understand why it was even necessary to begin with.

Chapter 2: The History of The Theory

In life it is very rare that a theory will go unchallenged and The Lines of Seth is no exception. The opposing theory is known as The Angel Theory, which states that the sons of God were really angels, the daughters of men are human women in general, and the giants were genetic hybrids known as the *nephilim*. Of the two theories, one of them is fully backed by the Bible and one is not. One of them was commonly accepted as strong Biblical doctrine and the other was not. One of them is supported by historical testimony and one is not. One of them is considered to be heresy and the other is not. It is up to us to determine which one of these theories fits into which category.

The Origin of The Theory

Simeon Bar Yochai, also known as Rashbi was a 1st Century A.D. *tannaic* sage that rose to importance after the year 70 A.D. The Hebrew word tanna means, to repeat what one was taught, which is the origin of the word *tannaic*. The actual *tannaic* doctrine was not written down until 70-200 A.D. in their holy book know as the *Mishnah*. According to tannaic belief, Moses received the written law on Sinai as well as the oral law, which until the writing of the *Mishnah*, was only passed on orally through tradition. Unfortunately, the *Tanakh* (Old Testament) has no record of such an event.

Simon Bar Yochai was a disciple of Rabbi Akiva and is believed to have authored the Zohar, which is the main portion of the Kabbalah. The *Zohar* is a group of books that which provide commentary on the mysticism of the Torah (Genesis - Deuteronomy).[1] In a nutshell, the *Zohar* is considered to be an elaboration on the Torah. From the very beginning, many Jewish scholars were skeptical of the *Zohar* because it was discovered by only one person and only makes references to historical events that occur after the period in which it is claimed to have been written.[2]

---

[1] Scholem, Gershom and Melila Hellner-Eshed. "Zohar." Encyclopaedia Judaica. Ed. Michael Berenbaum and Fred Skolnik. Vol. 21. 2nd ed. Detroit: Macmillan Reference USA, 2007. 647-664. Gale Virtual Reference Library. Gale.
[2] Jacobs, Joseph; Broydé, Isaac. "Zohar". *Jewish Encyclopedia*. Funk & Wagnalls Company.

> "A story tells that after the death of Moses de Leon, a rich man of Avila named Joseph offered Moses' widow (who had been left without any means of supporting herself) a large sum of money for the original from which her husband had made the copy. She confessed that her husband himself was the author of the work. She had asked him several times, she said, why he had chosen to credit his own teachings to another, and he had always answered that doctrines put into the mouth of the miracle-working Shimon bar Yochai would be a rich source of profit. The story indicates that shortly after its appearance the work was believed by some to have been written by Moses de Leon."[3]

The same Simeon Bar Yochai was believed to be a miracle worker and an exorcist, and it is also believed that it was he that first pronounced a curse on any Jew teaching The Angel Theory of Genesis 6. Simeon Bar Yochai believed that the sons of God referred to the Godly line of Seth and not to angels.

A History of Rejection

Almost right from the beginning The Lines of Seth Theory was challenged and rejected. The first person believed to completely reject the Lines of Seth teaching was Trypho the Jew. It is Justin Martyr (103-165 A.D.) that wrote of Trypho in his work, Dialogue With Trypho. Justin Martyr also rejected the Lines of Seth interpretation as an explanation of the events in Genesis 6. The next major rejection of The Lines of Seth Theory came from Rashi (1040 – 1105 A.D.). Rashi is considered to be "the father of all commentaries" that followed his comprehensive commentaries on both the Talmud and the Tanakh. His works are considered to be the centerpiece of contemporary Jewish study.

> "Another explanation of *b'nai ha elohim* : They are the angels who go as messengers of G-d; they, too, intermingled with them." – Rashi, Commentary: Bereishis 6:2 (Genesis 6:2)

---

[3] Jacobs, Joseph; Broydé, Isaac. "Zohar". *Jewish Encyclopedia*. Funk & Wagnalls Company.

In addition to the above section of text, Rashi also described the giants as "the men that devastated the world." He directly links the corruption of all flesh and the wrath of God to these giants that walked the earth in the time of Enosh and Cain. Nahmanides (1194 – 1270) was a leading Jewish scholar, rabbi, philosopher, physician, Kabbalist, and commentator. In his work, *Torat ha Adam*, he mocks those philosophers that pretend to have knowledge of the essence of God and angels, but do not fully understand their own bodies, which as we will see later, is one of the arguments put forth by The Lines of Seth Theory. There are several other notable names that have rejected The Lines of Seth Theory:

1. Pseudo-Clementine
2. Martin Luther
3. Athenagoras
4. Clement of Alexandria
5. Commondianus
6. Flavius Josephus
7. Tertullian
8. Philo Judaeus
9. John Wycliffe
10. Iranaeus
11. Lactantius

Even though the theory was widely rejected by many who were considered to be important scholars and philosophers, it was also embraced by many influential people as well.

A History of Acceptance

Shortly after the death of Simon Bar Yochai, a man by the name of Sextus Julius Africanus (c.160 – c.240 A.D.) started teaching the Lines of Seth view of Genesis Chapter 6, and it was he that helped it gain popularity within the Church. In the early history of the Catholic Church, it was considered heresy to challenge any accepted doctrine of the Catholic Church, so the Angel Theory slowly began to move underground. Although it was Africanus that popularized the theory, there were others that helped push it as the new accepted Church doctrine.

• Cyril of Alexandria

- St. Augustine

In his attempt to explain the events being reported in his time, St. Augustine (354 - 430 A.D.) drew from his belief in The Lines of Seth and made the following statement:

> "There is, too, a very general rumor, which many have veri-fied by their own experience, or which trustworthy persons who have heard the experience of others corroborate, that sylvans and fauns, who are commonly called incubi, had often made wicked assaults upon women." - St. Augustine, The City of God

Almost 1,000 years after the death of Africanus, The Lines of Seth Theory was once again reinforced by an important Catholic priest. Thomas Aquinas (1225 - 1274 A.D.) was a Catholic priest from the Dominican Order. Many theologians consider him to be a very important part of Church history, and he whole heartedly supported The Lines of Seth Theory. One of the lesser known facts about Aquinas is that he was a bit of an extremist in his beliefs. He believed in trying to convert people to Christianity through peace, but if that was ineffective, the use of violent coercion was acceptable. Then there were his views on heresy:

> "With regard to heretics two points must be observed: one, on their own side; the other, on the side of the Church. On their own side there is the sin, whereby they deserve not only to be separated from the Church by excommunication, but al-so to be severed from the world by death. For it is a much graver matter to corrupt the faith which quickens the soul, than to forge money, which supports temporal life. Where-fore if forgers of money and other evil-doers are forthwith condemned to death by the secular authority, much more reason is there for heretics, as soon as they are convicted of heresy, to be not only excommunicated but even put to death. On the part of the Church, however, there is mercy which looks to the conversion of the wanderer, wherefore she condemns not at once, but "after the first and second admo-nition," as the Apostle directs: after that, if he is yet stub-born, the Church no longer hoping for his conversion, looks to the salvation of others, by excommunicating him and separat-ing him from the Church, and furthermore delivers him to the

secular tribunal to be exterminated thereby from the world by death."[4] - Thomas Aquinas

As far as Aquinas was concerned, heresy was punishable by death, but what exactly is heresy? In short, heresy is any belief that goes against Church tradition. Thomas considered the Angel view of Genesis 6 to be heresy. Although Aquinas maintained an extremist position on heresy, he actually walked a fine line in an attempt to make sense of something that was being widely reported during his life.

> "Still if some are occasionally begotten from demons, it is not from the seed of such demons, nor from their assumed bodies, but from the seed of men taken for the purpose; as when the demon assumes first the form of a woman, and afterwards of a man; just as they take the seed of other things for other generating purposes."[5] - Thomas Aquinas

Although he was clearly a supporter of the Lines of Seth Theory, he did not completely dismiss the idea of hybrid offspring. He simply found another way to explain the events in Genesis 6 and his time by finding a way around the issue of sexual intercourse between human women and fallen angels.

The Breakdown

As we dig into the history of the Lines of Seth Theory, we find that the interpretation of Noah's flood is a very important issue, because every important person linked to the Church has chosen a position on the Genesis 6 controversy. The reason for this is because the interpretation of the events in Noah's time will set the foundation for most of the Old Testament, portions of the New Testament, and it is the key to understanding much of end time Bible prophecy. The position that someone chooses to take will ultimately affect how they view God, the Bible, and prophecy in general.

---

[4] *Summa*, II-II, Q.11, art.3
[5] Aquinus, Thomas (1265-1274), Summa Theologica

Chapter 3: The Sons of God

As we learned previously, it is the position of The Lines of Seth Theory that the sons of God refer to the "Godly line of Seth". This reference in the Bible is of such vast importance that it even extends beyond a Church issue into the modern secular world. There are generally three interpretations given to Genesis 6:1-4 concerning the sons of God:

1. The Lines of Seth: Sons of God = Seth's Line
2. The Angels View: Sons of God = Fallen Angels
3. The Secular View: Sons of God = Aliens

These are the three contending views that are embraced by every person that gives any credibility to the Biblical narrative. When we are faced with opposing interpretations of scripture, it is important to let scripture guide us toward the truth by putting away bias and tradition, and begin by stripping everything down to the core elements. There is a very easy way of doing this.

1. Consult the Strong's Concordance for the original language and definition.
2. Use the Bible to locate verses where the same word or phrase is used.
3. Read the verses in context.
4. Compare the context of all verses involved.

By following the above process we can safely separate what is true from what is false. What we will do in this chapter is follow this four part process in an effort to piece together what the Bible is actually referring to when it mentions "the sons of God."

Step 1: Consulting The Strong's

When we use the Strong's Concordance to find the original wording of the text, we discover that the Hebrew phrase is *"b'nai ha elohim"*. It is important to note that certain manuscripts and authors will render the spelling different, but it refers to the same sons of God. The most common renderings are the following:

- *ben elohim*

11

- *b'nai ha elohim*
- *bene ha'elohim*
- *bar elohim*

There may be other variations, but the exact spelling is of less importance than the actual interpretation. Let's start by addressing the first part of the phrase, which is the Hebrew word *ben* or *b'nai*. The word has several meaning and can refer to any of the following:

- Son
- Grandson
- Male Descendant

The next word we need to deal with is the Hebrew word "*elohim*". This is the word which has caused so much division over the interpretation of the passage. It is commonly taught that the word "*elohim*" means God, but that is not always the case. It is actually used in two different ways in the Bible. One is to refer to God, the creator of the universe, and the other is to refer to the gods as a way of referencing fallen angels. After completing step one, it is still unclear as to which position is correct and Biblical.

Step 2: Locating The Verses

In this step we need to locate all of the places in the Bible where the phrase "sons of God" is used. Once we find those verses, we need to repeat Step 1 to make sure we are indeed viewing the phrase "*b'nai ha elohim*." Once we establish that we are indeed looking at the same exact phrase, we need to list the verses in which that phrase occurs. If it is a Hebrew phrase, it will be limited to the Old Testament, as far as wording is concerned. After doing a little bit of searching, we find that the exact phrase "*b'nai ha elohim*" appears only five times in the Old Testament:

- Genesis 6:2
- Genesis 6:4
- Job 1:6
- Job 2:1
- Job 38:7
- Daniel 3:25*

12

The reason we need to do this is because Hebrew is a much more precise language than English. Many of the verses that are taken out of context in English cannot be taken out of context when referring to the original Hebrew. While that is not always the case, it is usually a safe way of hunting down the true intention behind the scriptures. Now that Step 2 is complete, we can move on to the next step in the process.

Step 3: Reading For Context

When reading, it is important to read the entire chapter for the complete context. It is unwise to build an entire doctrine based on a single verse that may be taken out of context. For the purposes of space in this book, only the verses in question will be quoted. Because it is Genesis 6:2 and 4 that are in question, we will be referring to the context of the other verses to determine what the Bible is referring to.

> "Now there was a day when the sons of God came to present themselves before the LORD, and Satan came also among them." - Job 1:6

By examining the above verse in detail we will be able to make several very important leaps in our progress. There are several things we need to take into account when reading this verse in Job.

1. This event is taking place after the flood.
2. The sons of God are presenting themselves before the Lord.
3. Satan comes with them.

Once again, we are going to consult the Strong's to understand what the sons of God are actually doing. The Hebrew word for present is *yatsab*, which means to stand or to take a stand. This was not just a presentation of some kind, the sons of God were coming to stand before the Lord and Satan is among them.

> "Again there was a day when the sons of God came to present themselves before the LORD, and Satan came also among them to present himself before the LORD." - Job 2:1

Again, we encounter the same wording and the same event, during which, Satan comes with them again. Because this event occurs twice, there are several possibilities as to what is going on.

1. Satan is not one of the sons of God, but is timing his appearance to coincide with their presentation.
2. The sons of God have an appointed time to stand before God.
3. Satan is counted as one of the sons of God and his presence is used to connect them to the fallen angel.

While this is still inconclusive, it does connect the fallen adversary of God to the sons of God in some way. There is one more verse that we need to examine before we can begin to form a Biblical position on the matter.

> "When the morning stars sang together, and all the sons of God shouted for joy?" - Job 38:7

By reading the above chapter in context, we find that God is questioning Job about the creation of the earth. In the first six verses, God is addressing the events preceding the creation of the earth, but more specifically the laying of the cornerstone. For those that are not familiar with construction, the laying of a cornerstone usually represents the starting place of the building to be constructed. In the verse above, God is informing Job that the sons of God shouted for Joy during this event. There are several more conclusions that we can make based on the context of these verses.

*   The sons of God existed before earth was created.
*   The sons of God saw the creation of earth.
*   The sons of God are not humans.

Finally, there is an Aramaic phrase in the book of Daniel that is equivalent to the Hebrew phrase *"b'nai ha elohim"*. In Daniel 3:25, the phrase used is *"bar elah"*, which is translated as "son of God".

> "He answered and said, Lo, I see four men loose, walking in the midst of the fire, and they have no hurt; and the form of the fourth is like the Son of God." - Daniel 3:25

Depending on which version you choose to read, it is sometimes translated as "a son of God", but it is the terminology used in the Aramaic that is important. If we read this entire story in the book of Daniel and keep it in context, we know that only three humans were thrown into the furnace by Nebuchadnezzar. It is the gentile king Nebuchadnezzar that recognizes the fourth as someone that is not human. In fact, it is he that reveals the nature of the fourth person in the fire.

> "Then Nebuchadnezzar spake, and said, Blessed be the God of Shadrach, Meshach, and Abednego, **who hath sent his angel**, and delivered his servants that trusted in him, and have changed the king's word, and yielded their bodies, that they might not serve nor worship any god, except their own God."
> – Daniel 3:28

In the above verse, we clearly read that Nebuchadnezzar calls this fourth person an angel. Now that we have completed this step, we can move on to the fourth and final step in the process.

Step 4: Comparing The Text

Now that we have taken the necessary steps to isolate the verses and wording in question, we need to make a comparison of the texts to determine how the terminology is used. When we compare Job 1, 2, 38, and Daniel 3, we find that the phrases *b'nai ha elohim* (Hebrew) and *bar elah* (Aramaic) are all associated with angels. Because four out of six references are crystal clear references to angels, the law of interpretation dictates that we remain consistent when we encounter the same phrase elsewhere in the text.

> "But if he will not hear thee, then take with thee one or two more, that in the mouth of two or three witnesses every word may be established." – Matthew 18:16

If the words in Genesis 6 are not enough to establish the identity of the sons of God, then we also have the witness of Job and Daniel who use the phrase in the same manner, using two different languages (Hebrew and Aramaic). This is why comparing the text is so important. Without the comparison it is easy to fall victim to misinterpretation and misapplication of scripture.

15

The Breakdown

When we compare the verses that deal with the specific phrase, "the sons of God", we find that they consistently refer to as angels. If we let the Bible change our beliefs, we do not need to change the Bible to fit our beliefs. Without any evidence to the contrary, the only way the sons of God can be interpreted are as angels. By avoiding this interpretation we are in fact ignoring the evidence found in the word of God in favor of our own interpretation. That line of thinking is prideful, arrogant, and non-Biblical.

It is at this point the The Lines of Seth Theory begins to fall apart and one must choose whether or not they want to stick to the Biblical narrative or to rely on the traditional misinterpretation of events. However, The Lines of Seth Theory may still have a leg to stand on. In the next chapter we will investigate the phrase "daughters of men" and it's relation to non-believers in scripture.

Chapter 4: The Daughters of Men

Now that we have examined how the phrase "sons of God" is used in the Old Testament, we need to find out what the phrase, "daughters of men" refers to. According to The Lines of Seth Theory, the phrase is a way to refer to the unbelieving line of Cain, and in some cases, unbelievers in general. In this chapter we will be following the same process that we used in the last chapter.

Step 1: Consulting The Strong's

In the Strong's Concordance, the phrase "daughters of men" is the Hebrew phrase, *"benoth Adam"*. First we will deal with the Hebrew word "benoth", which can mean the following:

- Daughter
- Granddaughter
- Female Descendant

The next word we need to define is *"Adam"*. It is commonly taught that the word Adam just means "man", but it can also be defined as follows:

- Man
- Mankind
- Mortal

It is also important to understand that the Hebrew word *Adam* is also a proper noun that can be used as a name. When we consider it as a proper noun, we are faced with two possible translations of the Hebrew phrase *"benoth adam"*:

1. Daughters of Men
2. Daughters of Adam

Now that we have used the Strong's Concordance to determine howthe phrase was interpreted, our next step is to locate the Bible verses that use the "phrase daughters of men" so that we can compare them for context.

Step 2: Locating The Verses

After running a quick search for the phrase "daughters of men", we find that it only occurs three times in scripture. Two of the three times it appears in the verses that we are attempting to interpret.

- Genesis 6:2
- Genesis 6:4
- Genesis 24:13

In both Genesis 6:2 and Genesis 6:4, the Hebrew phrase is *"benoth Adam"*. However, in Genesis 24:13, the Hebrew phrase is *"benoth ish"*. Both *Adam* and *ish* are used throughout the Bible to refer to men or mankind in a general sense. We will see why this is important as we make our way through the rest of this book.

Step 3: Reading For Context

When we read the above verses for context we find that Genesis 24:13 definitely refers to mankind in general, and Genesis 6:2 and 4 possibly refer to mankind in general or Adam specifically. It is important that we understand the context of these verses because they will play a vital role in figuring out what is actually going on in Genesis 6.

Step 4: Comparing The Text

Now that we have the context of all of the verses in question, we can compare them. When we do we find that the usage of the words *Adam* and *ish* exclude them from referring to anyone or anything other than mankind in general or in the case of *Adam*, Adam specifically. There is also another problem we run into if we apply The Lines of Seth interpretation to the word *Adam*.

> "And it came to pass, when men began to multiply on the face of the earth, and daughters were born unto them..." - Genesis 6:1

18

In this verse we again encounter the word *Adam* (men), which according to The Lines of Seth Theory is really a reference to Cain. The verse literally reads, "when *Adam* began to multiply on the face of the earth." Moses, inspired by the Holy Spirit, chose to use the word Adam instead of the word *ish* to tell this story, which means there is a reason behind it being told in such a manner. Our job as students of the Bible is to figure exactly why Genesis 6 continues to reference Adam and not Cain or Seth.

The Sons of Men

Because the phrase *"benoth adam"* only appears once in scripture, it is necessary for us to look at a similar Hebrew phrase. The phrase "sons of men" that occurs twenty one times in the Old Testament and two times in the New Testament.

Ben *Ish* (sons of men) - Hebrew

1. Psalm 4:2

Ben *Adam* (sons of men) - Hebrew

2. Psalm 31:19
3. Psalm 33:13
4. Psalm 57:4
5. Psalm 58:1
6. Psalm 145:12
7. Proverbs 8:31
8. Ecclesiastes 2:3
9. Ecclesiastes 2:8
10. Ecclesiastes 3:10
11. Ecclesiastes 3:18
12. Ecclesiastes 3:19
13. Ecclesiastes 8:11
14. Ecclesiastes 9:3
15. Ecclesiastes 9:12
16. Isaiah 52:14
17. Jeremiah 32:19
18. Daniel 10:16
19. Joel 1:12
20. Micah 5:7

Ben *Enash* (sons of men) - Aramaic

21. Daniel 5:21

19

Huios Anthropos (sons of men) - Greek

22. Mark 3:28
23. Ephesians 3:5

The reason that all twenty three references are grouped based on terminology is so that we can isolate the language closest to that found in Genesis 6. Once we separate these verses, we see that nineteen out of twenty three uses of the phrase are a close match, based on their use of the word *Adam*.

If the belief that unbelievers were referred to as "sons of men" has any merit to it, we also have to call into question two major Biblical figures. Both Ezekiel and Jesus were referred to as "son of man", and according to The Lines of Seth Theory, that phrase is used to designate non-believers from believers. Were Ezekiel and Jesus unbelievers? We know from scripture that they were clearly believers, one of whom was God in the flesh, so the teaching that this phrase is a designation for unbelievers is proven to be false when we use scripture as our guide.

The Dilemma of Seth

If The Lines of Seth Theory is to be given any merit at all, we would need to be able to locate at least one verse that refers to Seth or his lineage as "the sons of God". Seth is only mentioned eight times in the Bible, but not a single verse refers to him as godly or the son of God.

- Genesis 4:25
- Genesis 4:26
- Genesis 5:3
- Genesis 5:4
- Genesis 5:6
- Genesis 5:7
- Genesis 5:8
- Luke 3:38

In fact, once we begin digging into scripture, we find that the only mention of Seth outside of Genesis chapters 4 and 5 occurs in Luke, in which he is referred to as "the son of Adam".

20

> "Which was the son of Enos, which was the son of Seth, which was the **son of Adam**, which was the son of God." - Luke 3:38

Here we see Luke refer to Adam as "the son of God", but why not Seth, if Genesis 6 is really referring to the Sethites? The answer seems to be that neither Seth nor his descendants were referred to as the sons of God.

The Breakdown

Once again, by following a proven method for correctly interpreting scripture, we find that everything is not how it is presented to be when it comes to The Lines of Seth teaching. In order to accept the theory, one must completely ignore all of the example provided in scripture and choose to interpret the text however they see fit. Private interpretation is the cause for many of the false doctrines that we see floating around within the church, and simply put, The Lines of Seth Theory is one of those false doctrines that should be considered heresy.

21

Chapter 5: The Traditions of Men

Now that we have done our research into this traditional teaching, we need to understand why it is false, and considered by many to be heresy. When we can adequately explain why it is not true, we are better able to share with others in an intelligent and coherent manner.

> "Making the word of God of none effect through your tradition, which ye have delivered: and many such like things do ye." - Mark 7:13

According to the word of God, it is the traditions of men that make His word ineffective. Throughout this book we have looked at what the scriptures say in English, Hebrew, and Greek. What we have found is that The Lines of Seth Theory has no scriptural backing whatsoever, which lands it in the category of being just another tradition of men that is making the word of God ineffective. The reason that this particular doctrine is so vital is because it is the key to understanding much of the Old Testament and several prophecies concerning the end of the age in the New Testament.

The Sons of God

As we have learned, the Hebrew phrase *"b'nai ha elohim"* is only used in the Old Testament to refer to angels. According to those that hold to The Lines of Seth teaching, this same phrase refers to the "sons of Seth". There are a few problems with this interpretation:

1. Seth is never referred to as elohim.
2. Elohim is never referred to as Seth.
3. Elohim is only translated as God/gods.

Because of these facts, we cannot interpret the phrase "sons of God" as a reference to the sons of Seth. In addition to the above fact, Genesis 6 contains no references at all to the name Seth in any part of the text. In order to hold the belief that the sons of God were actually the sons of Seth, we have to disregard scripture and add the reference to Seth in for ourselves.

The Daughters of Men

When we breakdown the phrase *"benoth Adam"* we find that the word Adam is only used as a proper noun or translated as the plural for mankind. When we examine The Lines of Seth interpretation, we find similar problems to those found with the translation "sons of God".

1. Cain is never referred to as Adam.
2. Adam is never referred to as Cain.
3. Adam is only translated as Adam/men/mankind.

Once again, the facts prove that we cannot interpret Adam to mean Cain. If we are to accept The Lines of Seth theory, we will have to add Cain to Genesis 6, because it does not appear in the text.

The Line of Righteousness

According to The Lines of Seth doctrine, Seth's entire line was righteous, even though this cannot be found in scripture. There are also several Biblical facts that point to this being a false interpretation of scripture:

The Salvation of Noah - With the exception of Noah and his family, the entire lineage of Seth was wiped out in the flood. If the entire lineage of Seth was righteous, that would mean that God destroys both the righteous and the wicked without prejudice. This action is contrary to what we know from scripture, and that is God will not destroy the righteous with the wicked.

The Daughters of God - According to Genesis 6 it was the sons of God that began taking the daughters of men, and making wives of them. There is no mention of the daughters of God taking part in these events.

The Sons of Men - Much like the above stated problem, the sons of men are not mentioned as taking part in these events.

According to the Lines of Seth theory, it was the sons of God (Seth's Line) that began taking wives of the daughters of men (Cain's Line). The theory teaches that this mixing was forbidden by God, but if that is true, then it is the line of Seth that is responsible for initiating rebellion against God's law. Rebellion against God is not an action we would expect from a righteous line of people.

There are those that put forth the argument that all believers are considered to be the "sons of God", and so Genesis 6 simply refers to believers. Once again, when we apply the lens of scripture, we find a completely different story.

> "But as many as received him, to them gave he power to become the sons of God, even to them that believe on his name:" - John 1:12

There are only two ways to become a son of God. One way is by being a direct creation of God, and the other way is receiving Christ. If Seth was not a direct creation by God and Christ had not yet been resurrected, how did Seth's line come to be called the sons of God? Something else that is worthy of pointing out is that if the phrase referred to the sons of Seth, it means that they initiated the disobedience to God, not Cain's line. The scripture indicates that the sons of God took wives of all that "they chose". There are also two more questions that arise from this theory:

- Why did Seth's entire lineage except for Noah's family die in the flood?
- Why were they in the company of Satan in Job Chapters 1 and 2?

We can clearly see that the evidence so far argues against the sons of God actually being the sons of Seth. Another major stumbling block for the theory is lack of scriptural support. Seth may have been the replacement for Abel's death, but nowhere does it say that his entire line was godly. Another verse that adds a nail to this coffin is found in Hebrews:

> "For verily he took not on him the nature of angels; but he took on him the seed of Abraham." - Hebrews 2:16

Here the Bible refers to the seed of Abraham, but we do not assume that the Bible really means someone other than Abraham, so why do some people make the same assumption about Genesis 6? We know the Bible is talking about the Nation of Israel specifically. Why do some try to change the Word of God to fit their own personal beliefs? The Bible says what it means and means what it says. When it refers to the sons of Elohim (God), it is not referring to anyone other than God. When it says daughters of Adam, it is not referring to anyone other than Adam. When it says Abraham, it is not referring to anyone other than Abraham.

God's Word	Man's Word
Sons of God	Sons of Seth
Daughters of Adam	Daughters of Cain

"Add thou not unto his words, lest he reprove thee, and thou be found a liar." - Proverbs 30:6

Genealogy of Seth

Seth is the son that God blessed Adam and Eve with after Cain killed Abel. There is no scriptural reference to Seth's line being godly, but it seems to be an invention of man to twist the scripture to fit their beliefs instead of twisting their beliefs to fit scripture. Let's take a look at Seth's line starting with Adam and concluding with Noah.

- Adam - Man
- Seth - Appointed
- Enos - Mortal
- Cainan - Sorrow
- Mahalaleel - Blessed God
- Jared - Come Down
- Enoch - Teaching, Educated, or Dedicated
- Methuselah - His Death Shall Bring
- Lamech - Despairing, Poor, or Made Low
- Noah - Rest or Comfort

We know that Seth's line is continued through Noah, Shem, Ham, and Japheth, but what we do not know is where their wives came from. It is possible that the sons of Noah married the daughters of Cain, but that would make the flood pointless to all that hold this belief. If God's intentions were to wipe out the earth because of this mixing, that means He would have failed by only saving a group of people in mixed marriages. There is no Biblical evidence to support the theory that Seth's line could not mix with the line of Cain. It is entirely possible that Noah, Shem, Ham, and Japheth had wives that came from the line of Cain, but again, the Bible is completely silent on the issue. Genesis 4:26 also offers us an interesting insight to something else about Seth's line.

"And to Seth, to him also there was born a son; and he called his name Enos: then began men to call upon the name of the LORD." - Genesis 4:26

Supporters of the Lines of Seth view use this verse to support the theory that Seth's line was godly because Enos began calling upon the name of the Lord. If that is true, who did Adam, Cain, Abel, and Seth call upon?

> The traditional Jewish interpretation of this verse, though, implies that it marked the beginning of idolatry, i.e. that men started dubbing "Lord" things that were mere creatures. This is because the previous generations, notably Adam, had already "begun calling upon the name of the Lord", which forces us to interpret *huchal* not as "began" but as the homonym "profaned". In this light, Enos suggests the notion of a humanity (Enoshut) thinking of itself as an absolute rather than in relation to God.[1]

As we start to unravel the myth of Seth's line being righteous, we begin to see that this was not the traditional Jewish belief. Seth's son Enos is viewed as the first idolater and the rest of Seth's sons initiate disobedience to God by making wives of Cain's daughters, if we hold to that view. Are these the actions that we would expect from a godly line?

The Line of Evil

According to the Bible the sons of God took women of their own choosing. This implies, and is backed by cultural tradition, that the women had no say in the matter. If this is true, then it is not the women from the line of Cain that are disobeying, and there is no mention of the sons of Cain taking part in these forbidden marriages. In addition to these facts, the Bible gives us a unique look into Cain's relationship with God.

> "And Adam knew Eve his wife; and she conceived, and bare Cain, and said, I have gotten a man from the LORD." - Genesis 4:1

The reason that this verse is so important is because there are people that twist scripture and make the claim that Cain is the son of Eve and Satan, which is not supported by the Bible at all. That theory is known

---

[1] http://en.wikipedia.org/wiki/Enos_(Bible)

as Serpent Seed and is covered in depth in my book <u>The Serpent Seed:</u>
<u>Debunked.</u> There is a clear order of events listed in the above verse:

1. Adam has sex with his wife.
2. Cain is conceived.
3. Cain is born.
4. Cain is a man.
5. Cain is from the Lord.

According to the Bible, Cain is not the evil hybrid son of Satan, but a
fully human male, which makes him subject to a sinful nature. Because
all men are capable of sin, Cain was overcome by jealousy when his
sacrifice was not accepted by God.

> "But unto Cain and to his offering he had not respect. And Cain was
> very wroth, and his countenance fell." - Genesis 4:5

The phrase "very wroth" is the Hebrew word *charah*, which means:
to burn with anger. There are all kinds of reasons that people will offer
as to why Cain's offering was not accepted, but the only thing the Bible
tells us is that it was not right for some reason or another.

> "And the LORD said unto Cain, Why art thou wroth? and why is thy
> countenance fallen? If thou doest well, shalt thou not be accepted?
> and if thou doest not well, sin lieth at the door. And unto thee shall
> be his desire, and thou shalt rule over him." - Genesis 4:6-7

The above verse is important because God is speaking directly to Cain
in an attempt to comfort him even after rejecting his offering. This
shows that there is a relationship with God in which they are on speaking terms. Many times this fact is neglected when the story of Cain and
Able is taught. Even after this talk with God, Cain is still made and kills
his brother.

> "And Cain talked with Abel his brother: and it came to pass, when
> they were in the field, that Cain rose up against Abel his brother, and
> slew him." - Genesis 4:8

The above verse is pretty straight forward in that Cain killed Abel.
Contrary to popular belief, there is no mention of a rock or the method
that Cain used to kill Abel, as is commonly taught and depicted. This is
Cain's only recorded sin in the Bible. As we continue reading, we encounter Cain's punishment for his sin.

> "And now art thou cursed from the earth, which hath opened her mouth to receive thy brother's blood from thy hand; When thou tillest the ground, it shall not henceforth yield unto thee her strength; a fugitive and a vagabond shalt thou be in the earth." - Genesis 4:11-12

The curse that God placed on Cain directly affected his livelihood. In Genesis 4:2 we learn that Cain was a tiller of the ground, and because of this curse he could no longer do what he was good at. In addition to him not being able to grow crops as he once did, he was cursed to be a fugitive and a vagabond, meaning he would constantly be on the run and not able to settle down. However, Cain spoke up and plead for a sentence that was less harsh.

> "And Cain said unto the LORD, My punishment is greater than I can bear. Behold, thou hast driven me out this day from the face of the earth; and from thy face shall I be hid; and I shall be a fugitive and a vagabond in the earth; and it shall come to pass, that every one that findeth me shall slay me." - Genesis 4:13-14

In our culture, repentance involves an apology or saying, "I repent", but that was not always the case in the past. All through the Bible we find that repentance was not the same as it is now, but involved the following actions as well:

- Dressing in sackcloth.
- Putting ashes on the head.
- Tearing of the clothes.

Based on the context and series of events, the above verses do indeed indicate that Cain was repenting for his actions. Notice that being hidden from God's face was never part of the curse. The hiding of the face was an acknowledgment of shame for wrongdoing. Once Cain says his part, God has compassion on him and does something unique that only occurs three times in all of scripture.

> "And the LORD said unto him, Therefore whosoever slayeth Cain, vengeance shall be taken on him sevenfold. And the LORD set a mark upon Cain, lest any finding him should kill him." - Genesis 4:15

Once again, we encounter a verse that has garnered all kinds of speculation from those that do not use the Strong's Concordance to verify the meaning of the Hebrew words used in this verse. There are those that believe that this mark was a curse and some go even further and say that this curse involved Cain's skin becoming black in order to promote racism.

As we examine the verse, we find that many of the false teachings involving the mark of Cain fall apart when compared to scripture. The first part of the verse reveals that God is promising to take sevenfold vengeance on anyone that kills Cain. The second half of the verse confirms that the mark of Cain was a positive thing because it only occurs three times in scripture:

1. Genesis 4:15
2. Ezekiel 9:4
3. Revelation 7:3

When we look at the examples in Ezekiel and Revelation, it is clear that God's mark was a visible sign of protection from death placed on the forehead. According to the Strong's Concordance, the word for "mark" used in Genesis 4:15 is as follows:

- *Oth*: a sign, pledge, promise, miracle, token

The Hebrew word *oth* in Genesis 4:15 is likely the origin of the English word "oath", which has the same definition. If can was as evil as he is made out to be, why would God place a protective mark on him? Cain's crime was an emotionally charged crime of passion, and even in our modern society we have laws concerning crimes of passion:

"A defendant's excuse for committing a crime due to sudden anger or heartbreak, in order to eliminate the element of "premeditation. This usually arises in murder or attempted murder cases, when a spouse or sweetheart finds his/her "beloved" having sexual intercourse with another and shoots or stabs one or both of the coupled pair."[2]

As we previously learned, Cain burned with anger because his offering was rejected by God. If the feeling of being betrayed by a spouse or lover can lead to a crime of passion, it is entirely reasonable to conclude that a face to face rejection by the Creator of the universe would definitely lead to a similar emotional reaction.

---

[2] http://legal-dictionary.thefreedictionary.com/crime+of+passion

Cain's response was definitely based on emotion, but it was still a punishable action. Because Cain was the first person to murder another person, his actions presented the opportunity for him to be the very first example of God's grace and mercy. As we continue reading, we find more evidence that the mark was not a curse.

> "And Cain went out from the presence of the LORD, and dwelt in the land of Nod, on the east of Eden. And Cain knew his wife; and she conceived, and bare Enoch: and he builded a city, and called the name of the city, after the name of his son, Enoch." - 4:16-17

In Genesis 4:11-12, part of Cain's curse was to be a fugitive and a vagabond. Before we continue, lets define those two words and see what insights can be gained when we compare them to scripture.

Fugitive: A person who is fleeing, from prosecution, intolerable circumstances, etc.[3]

Vagabond: Wandering from place to place without any settled home; nomadic.

Now that we have defined these two words, we can clearly see that Genesis 4:16-17 does not reflect these two portions of the original curse. God placing His mark on Cain allowed him to settle down, take a wife, have a son, and build a city. None of which would have been possible if these parts of the curse had not been lifted. When we look at the entire context of the story we see God's grace, mercy, and compassion on Cain, just as He has on all of us when we sin and repent.

What Is Repentance?

In order to make the argument that Cain repented, we need to once again look at the Biblical text for evidence. We briefly touched on the subject previously, but what exactly is repentance?

Repent: To feel sorry, self-reproachful, or contrite for past conduct; regret or be conscience-stricken about a past action, attitude, etc.[4]

---

[3] http://dictionary.reference.com/browse/fugitive

[4] http://dictionary.reference.com/browse/repent

Contrary to popular belief, repenting has nothing to do with the uttering of words, but with how someone feels emotionally about past actions. As previously touched upon, Cain hid his face from the Lord, which indicates the feeling of shame for his actions, which fits the definition for repentance.

The Mark of Cain

In order to make this theory to fit, those that hold this view need to make their own changes to words in the actual Biblical text. Cain killed Abel, so it is assumed that his entire line is ungodly, but God forgave Cain and placed a mark of protection on him. Contrary to popular belief, this mark was not the result of a curse (Genesis Chapter 4), but a sign of God's grace and mercy.

Cain seems to get a bad rap for his actions, but God forgave him. Not only did God forgive him, but also He placed a mark on Cain and promised to avenge him sevenfold (Genesis 4:15) if anyone killed him. This mark does not sound like the mark of a curse, but the mark of God's blessing. It is true that Cain made a mistake, but that does not make his entire line ungodly, as some would have us believe. Cain is a perfect example of God's grace and mercy. Let's look at what the Bible says about the people in Cain's lineage.

- Cain - Possession or Spear
- Enoch - Teaching, Educated, or Dedicated
- Irad - Donkey, City of Witness, or Fugitive
- Mehujael - Struck by God
- Methusael - Man Who Asked God
- Lamech - Despairing, Poor, or Made Low
- Jubal - Ram
- *Naamah (daughter) - Pleasant
- Tubal-Cain - Worldly Possession

This is the last mention of Cain's genealogy in the Bible, which becomes important in refuting the many false doctrines surrounding Cain's bloodline. Some scholars would have us believe that because Cain killed Abel, his entire line is cursed, but that simply is not true. The Bible does not make any reference to Cain's line being cursed or any commandment for them not to mix with Seth's line.

Logical Problems With The Theory

For The Lines of Seth Theory to hold up, one needs to add their personal opinion to the text and dismiss actual scripture. The following questions need to be answered if we are to accept the view that Cain's line was ungodly:

- Why were Seth's sons taking wives of their own choosing from the daughters of Cain?
- Why were Seth's sons disobeying a direct command of God if they were godly?
- Why not just say the sons of Seth and daughters of Cain, if that is what the text is referring to?

Seth's line is the one that seems to be acting against the will of God if we actually read the story. It seems as though the "daughters of Cain" had no say in the matter according to the text, and the sons of Cain did not participate in this event. Everyone in Cain's line seems to be completely innocent as far as the text of Genesis 6:1-4 is concerned. The facts seem to support the exact opposite of what the Lines of Seth Theory teaches. According to scripture, Cain's line seems to be neutral in these events and Seth's sons seem to initiate the defiance of God. The fact that innocent people die in the flood seems contrary to God's nature and the revelation that He will not destroy the good along with the evil when it comes to judgment (Genesis 18:25). According to Genesis 4:16 Cain went to the land of Nod to the east of Eden. Either Cain's daughters returned to Cain's original home or Seth's sons journeyed to Nod to seek out the daughters of Cain. The Bible seems to specifically point out the fact that Cain separated himself from the rest of his family before getting married and having children, further complicating the possibility that this event was just two groups of people mixing without permission.

Another problem with this theory is that Genesis 5:4 states that Adam had other sons and daughters. Why exactly would the sons of Seth specifically seek out the daughters of Cain and ignore the other women around them? Again, there are too many problems that arise when we try to manipulate the text in order to fit our view. If we hold to this particular view we are no long relying on scripture to shape our belief, but are actually preaching our own gospel. While we are on the subject of Cain, let's explore a few other false teachings about this man of God.

The Serpent Seed Theory

There is another belief that Eve had sex with Lucifer in the garden, and as a result conceived Cain. This is an extremely dangerous view because it requires you to put your word and belief above the Word of God. God knows in advance what people are going to say and do, so one only needs to look at the scripture to determine if what they are being taught is the truth.

> "Not as Cain, who was of that wicked one, and slew his brother. And wherefore slew he him? Because his own works were evil, and his brother's righteous." - 1 John 3:12

When we take one verse alone without comparing it to the rest of the Bible, we run the risk of taking things out of context. This is a perfect example of how someone can take a verse out of context and add their own story behind it. Cain being "of that wicked one" does not mean that the union of Eve and Lucifer conceived him. This is not consistent with scripture for three reasons:

- God has a history of destroying the half-breed angels/humans.
- God specifically puts a mark on Cain so that nobody would kill him.
- God promises to take sevenfold vengeance on anyone that does kill Cain.

All three of these are inconsistent with all of God's other commands concerning the offspring of fallen angels and humans. In order to clear up the confusion, we can turn to the words of Jesus concerning the Pharisees:

> "Ye are of your father the devil, and the lusts of your father ye will do. He was a murderer from the beginning, and abode not in the truth, because there is no truth in him. When he speaketh a lie, he speaketh of his own: for he is a liar, and the father of it." - John 8:44

Jesus calls the Pharisees sons of the devil, but He is not talking in a physical sense. In order to understand the context, we need to understand that this is an insult and not a genealogy.

> "But Elymas the sorcerer (for so is his name by interpretation) withstood them, seeking to turn away the deputy from the faith. Then Saul, (who also is called Paul,) filled with the Holy Ghost, set his eyes on him. And said, O full of all subtilty and all mischief, thou child of the devil, thou enemy of all righteousness, wilt thou not cease to pervert the right ways of the Lord." - Acts 13:8-10

Here again, Paul calls Elymas the child of the devil, but does Paul think the devil is literally Elymas' father? It is highly unlikely. Again, it is an insult for Jews who consider themselves to be people of God, to be called children of the devil. Thankfully Jesus puts this entire issue in plain language for us:

> "He that committeth sin is of the devil; for the devil sinneth from the beginning. For this purpose the Son of God was manifested, that he might destroy the works of the devil." - 1 John 3:8

As we can clearly see, whoever sins is considered to be "of the devil". In the same context, this is what John is saying about Cain in 1 John 3:12, but what proof do we have that Cain was not the son of Lucifer?

> "These were more noble than those in Thessalonica, in that they received the word with all readiness of mind, and searched the scriptures daily, whether those things were so." - Acts 17:11

Let's search our Bibles and see if these things are so. If Cain is the son of Lucifer our Bible should agree 100% with what is being taught, but if this view is wrong, the Bible will disagree with it 100%.

> "And Adam knew Eve his wife; and she conceived, and bare Cain, and said, I have gotten a man from the LORD." - Genesis 4:1

This single verse seems to slap the entire theory in the face. The verse gives us four elements that rule out Cain being the son of Lucifer:

- Adam and Eve are no longer in Eden.
- Adam has sex with Eve.
- Eve conceives after having sex with Adam.
- Eve declares that she received her son from the Lord.

The idea that Cain is the son of Lucifer is in direct conflict with the Word of God. Usually when something is in direct conflict with the Word of God, it is not of God. Man's theory says the following:

- Eve was in the Garden when she had sex with Lucifer.
- Eve conceived Cain as a result of this act.
- Eve's son is from Lucifer and not God.

Everything is in opposition to what the scripture tells us. Also make note that Eve specifically says that she received Cain from the Lord, but no such statement is made about Abel or Seth. It seems as though these exact words were put there for the purpose of refuting the belief that Cain was the son of the devil. This theory is arrogant and prideful because it puts the word of man above the Word of God. Be careful of anyone teaching this false view, and question everything else they teach from that point on.

God's Word	Man's Word
Adam + Eve = Cain	Lucifer + Eve = Cain
Cain conceived outside garden	Cain conceived inside garden.
Received a man from the Lord	Received a man from Lucifer

When we break down the differences between God's Word and man's word, we can clearly see if it lines up with scripture or not. If the words do not appear in the original Hebrew or Greek, the English translation does not make reference to it, and the Bible contradicts the idea, we can be assured that man is preaching his own gospel and not the Word of God.

"Beloved, believe not every spirit, but try the spirits whether they are of God: because many false prophets are gone out into the world." - 1 John 4:1

For a more in depth study on The Serpent Seed Theory, its origin, anti Semitic nature, and why it is false according to the Bible, please read The Serpent Seed: Debunked.

Men of God And Murder

Does murder negate us from becoming a man or woman of God? Those that view Cain as ungodly because he committed murder have not dug deep enough into scripture yet. Several of the men that God chooses to do His will, have murder in their background.

- Abraham - He took his trained servants and killed an army of men to get his nephew back. (Genesis 14:14-16)
- Simeon and Levi - They killed every single man in a city and took the women and children as slaves because the king raped their sister. The Levites eventually become the priests. (Genesis 34:25-29)
- Moses - He murdered an Egyptian and buried him in the sand so no one would know. (Exodus 2:12)
- David - He got another man's wife pregnant, and then murdered the man so no one would find out. (2 Samuel 11)

All of these men were still used by God even after they committed these sins. The lesson with Cain's sin is not that God will curse us forever, but that God is forgiving to the point that He will personally place His protection over us. The second lesson is that murder does not disqualify us from being a man or woman of God.

Does The Antichrist Come From Cain?

This is another one of those views that puts the pride of man above the Word of God. There are some that say the Antichrist can be traced through Cain's line, further adding to the false theory that Cain's line is ungodly. In order to believe that the Antichrist emerges from Cain's line, we have to take up the position that our own word is truth regardless of what the Bible says.

> "Which sometime were disobedient, when once the longsuffering of God waited in the days of Noah, while the ark was a preparing, wherein few, that is, eight souls were saved by water." - 1 Peter 3:20

Peter specifically states that only eight souls were saved. If we count, we know that they were Noah, Shem, Ham, Japheth, and all of their wives. Animals are never referred to as having souls. Furthermore, we have the following scripture to support what Peter said:

> "And every living substance was destroyed which was upon the face of the ground, both man, and cattle, and the creeping things, and the fowl of the heaven; and they were destroyed from the earth: and

> "Noah only remained alive, and they that were with him in the ark." - Genesis 7:23

The Bible specifically says that only Noah and those in the ark with him remained alive. If Cain's genealogy ends with the Great Flood, how is it then possible to trace the Antichrist through his lineage? If we are to buy into the Antichrist coming from the line of Cain, the following questions need to be answered:

- Is the Bible lying when it states that only eight people survived the flood?
- Are we willing to call God's Word a lie in order to make man's word correct?

> "Add thou not unto his words, lest he reprove thee, and thou be found a liar." - Proverbs 30:6

Are The Kenites Descendants of Cain?

The more we explore these false teachings about Cain, the stranger the ideas get. One such false idea is that Cain is the father of the Kenites and as such, the Kenites are cursed. Racist groups and individuals that propose the idea that the Kenites are either African or Jewish, depending on who is teaching this theory, usually hold this view. Genesis Chapter 4 is the only scriptural reference to Cain's genealogy. The flood in Genesis Chapter 6 wipes out all of mankind except Noah's family, as we have already discovered using the Bible. How is it possible that Cain fathered the Kenites if the Kenites are not mentioned until after the flood? According to the Bible, there is absolutely no truth to this belief.

The Kenites as a nation are mentioned exactly seven times in the Bible and not a single reference mentions them being the descendants of Cain. Associating them with Cain is man's doing in order to encourage racism and self-interest. When we look into the words of the Bible, we can actually trace the true origin of the Kenites.

Moses father in law Jethro was a Midianite and so was his other father in law Hobab. Hobab was referred to as "the son of Raguel the Midianite" (Numbers 10:29). In Judges 4:1 we find that Heber is of the children of Hobab, but he is referred to as a Kenite. If this is true, the Kenite line started with someone from the line of Hobab and not the line of Cain, as some would have us believe. Understanding the termi-nology of the time is very important when tracing genealogy. The words grandfather, grandmother, grandson, and granddaughter are never used in the Bible. Everyone is referred to as a father, mother, son, or daughter regardless of how many generations apart they are. Heber may have been Hobab's great grandson, great great grandson, or even farther in the generational line for all we know, but the Bible is 100% clear that the Kenites started with someone in the line of Hobab.

God's Grace and Mercy

Because Cain committed the first murder, many Christians view him and his entire lineage as evil and somehow disqualified from grace and mercy. Unfortunately, this tradition has been passed on as if is scrip-ture, even though scripture says the opposite. According to scripture:

> "Wherefore I say unto you, All manner of sin and blasphemy shall be forgiven unto men: but the blasphemy against the Holy Ghost shall not be forgiven unto men." - Matthew 12:31

If God does not change, then this New Testament verse would also apply to Cain. After thoroughly examining the text we find that there is absolutely no basis in assuming that Cain's entire line was evil or that the women in his line were referred to as "the daughters of men." The entire Lines of Seth Theory is a completely fabricated story that was created in an attempt to explain away what is known as the Angel Theory, which suggests that fallen angels had offspring with human women. Those that oppose the Angel Theory do not base their beliefs on actual scripture, but rely on tradition to make their case.

The Breakdown

After conducting a thorough examination of the scriptures in con-junction with a Strong's Concordance, one has to wonder how such a non-Biblical theory became so popular among so many Christians. In reality it is likely a combination of accepting tradition as scripture and failure to challenge a preacher about the doctrine that they are teach-ing. Often in church there is a herd mentality that encourages all at-tendees to follow all of the teaching without question. This is a tradition that needs to be broken within the body of Christ because it is not Biblical and it leads to non-Biblical doctrine being passed down.

 Minister Dante Fortson was born November 15, 1982 in Las Vegas, NV, to Pastor Perryetta Lacy. As a child, growing up in his grandparents' house, Minister Dante Fortson had many experiences that have helped shape his belief in God and the supernatural. As a result of a dream one night and hearing his name being called in the house the following morning, he was saved and baptized at a very young age.

In elementary school he would read about vampires, ghosts, and other supernatural phenomena every chance he had. As he neared the 8th grade, Minister Fortson developed a sudden interest in UFOs, aliens, and the occult. One night, after a seemingly failed attempt to channel what he believed to be extraterrestrials, a life changing demonic experience left him with a lasting fear of the dark and led him to start studying the Bible more intensely for an explanation of the events. It has been a little over a decade since Minister Fortson became a student of Bible prophecy. Now, considered by many to be an expert in demonology, angelology, and the supernatural, he freely shares his knowledge and experience with anyone seeking advice in spiritual matters.

His goal is to provide a place where people can turn to and get solid Biblical answers about their supernatural experiences without the fear of ridicule that is often times present in mainstream churches. Minister Fortson believes that having a strong Biblical foundation is the key to understanding what people label as supernatural events. It is his belief that the Bible is of supernatural origin and contains truthful explanations of supernatural events that have occurred throughout history.

If you have a question in regards to the supernatural, you can contact Minister Fortson by visiting his website and sending him an email.

www.MinisterFortson.com

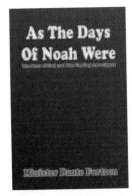

As The Days of Noah Were
The Sons of God and The Coming Apocalypse

What does the Bible really say about the last days on earth? Who were the sons of God? What were the strange beings known as the Nephilim? Did God really hide everything we need to know about the last days in the book of Genesis? Step by step we will journey through the days of Noah and piece together our coming future. We will explore stories from Sumer, Greece, and various other cultures to fill in the missing pieces to one of the biggest mysteries on our planet. Who were the sons of God and will they return?

"I recommend reading: 'As The Days of Noah Were', by Minister Dante Fortson. 'As The Days' is a well researched text, wonderfully fascinating. I've read a number of books on supernatural phenomenon - how such phenomenon manifests within our more understood physical reality - this book is among the best." - C. Heidt

"One thing I appreciate about this book (and Dante's ministry in general) is how he challenges believers to read the Scripture for themselves to verify what they're being taught and not just believe what they are taught because they're told it's true, when the teaching is nothing more than the traditions of men." - L. Holmes

"This book is amazing in its premise and conclusions. Very well researched and documented by the author. Literally, my view of the world and the Bible changed due to this book." - Stacey Harper

"After hundreds of hours of podcast listening to Dante and many other well educated hard working researchers, I found his book to be very well organized, full of vital information, and easy to read and understand. I learned a great deal more than I had previously digested from all the various podcasts and books which I'd poured through after my introduction to this "alternative" thinking which I know was brought to me by the Holy Spirit of God." - Christopher Moffitt

Beyond Flesh and Blood
The Ultimate Guide To Angels and Demons

Beyond Flesh and Blood: The Ultimate Guide To Angels and Demons goes far beyond the average Sunday School teaching on spiritual warfare. Minister Fortson takes an in depth look at the origin of both angels and demons, and attempts to answer the tough questions on the minds of many Christians.

1. When were angels created?
2. When did Lucifer rebel against God?
3. Where do angels fit into human history?
4. Are fallen angels and demons the same thing?
5. Were the gods of mythology really fallen angels?
6. What do angels have to do with modern UFO sightings?
7. Is our current scientific pursuit of transhumanism a spiritual issue?

These questions are just the beginning of the journey. As the book progresses, Minister Fortson tackles many other areas of the supernatural, such as the origin of ghosts, vampires, and our modern obsession with UFOs and aliens. You will also discover what our modern pursuit of creating hybrids has in common with various ancient mythologies from around the world, and the possible origin of these pursuits.

Throughout the book, Minister Fortson explores historical text from many different cultures and belief systems in order to find out if the Hebrews were the only culture to encounter both angels and demons. The Bible tells us that our war is not with flesh and blood, but what does that statement really mean? Is the spiritual war crossing over into the physical realm? One thing is for sure, after you read this book, you will never look at the world we live in the same again.

27193669R10030

Made in the USA
Lexington, KY
31 October 2013